OUR
EVANGELICAL
FAITH

Victor Shepherd

OUR EVANGELICAL FAITH

VICTOR SHEPHERD

CLEMENTS PUBLISHING
Toronto, Ontario

For
Caleb, Emma, Sam and Matthew,
grandchildren whom the evangelical faith
— owned, cherished and kept —
will find among "the great cloud of witnesses."
(Hebrews 11:1)

Published 2006 by Clements Publishing
6021 Yonge St., Box 213, Toronto, ON M2M 3W2 Canada
Web: www.clementspublishing.com
E-mail: info@clementspublishing.com

Edited by Bill Fledderus

Library and Archives Canada Cataloguing in Publication

Shepherd, Victor A., 1944-
Our evangelical faith / Victor A. Shepherd.

ISBN 1-894667-84-0

1. Evangelicalism. I. Title.

BR1640.S55 2006   230'.04624   C2006-900967-8

CONTENTS

FOREWORD

Over the years Canada has become a more religiously diverse society. While the majority of Canadians continue to profess belief in God, call themselves Christians and identify with a denomination, a recent poll indicates that 70 percent also believe that new forms of spirituality are replacing traditional, organized religion. Much larger "spirituality" sections now replace the "religion" section in bookstores, and spirituality is a common theme in magazines and on TV talk shows.

Within this context, it is vital to be rooted in sound doctrine. For evangelical Christians, foremost are the centrality of the cross in which we find forgiveness for sin; the vitality of a personal relationship with Jesus Christ and a life lived as his followers; the authority of the Scriptures in life; and the importance of sharing one's faith in word and deed with our neighbours. Evangelicalism can be characterized as a movement of Christianity that is as old as Christianity itself. And within a modern context Evangelicals express their faith within a plurality of denominations and churches, while challenging new forms of spirituality and liberal theology. Foremost, Evangelicals continue to celebrate the truth of Christian faith in all spheres of life—the Lordship of Christ.

When we decided to run a series of articles on the Evangelical Fellowship of Canada's statement of faith in *Faith Today* magazine, our first thought was to approach Victor Shepherd.

Shepherd writes with the precision of a theologian and the heart of a pastor. His understanding of evangelical belief has been tested and refined over the years through a journey of defending and promoting orthodoxy and maintaining a clear evangelical witness against theological liberalism. The result is an explication of evangelical belief whose brevity and clarity is as compelling as it is instructive.

I highly commend this book to you. It will serve to explain what it means to be evangelical in faith and it will foster and deepen the dedication of Evangelicals to the core commitments we share.

Bruce Clemenger, President
The Evangelical Fellowship of Canada

INTRODUCTION

WHAT IS AN EVANGELICAL?

What's the point of doctrine? Why do all evangelical organizations insist on doctrinal affirmations?

It's because Jesus Christ is *real*. This bedrock conviction has characterized Christians from the apostolic era to the present. Jesus Christ is true—better, He is *Truth*. What His followers confess about Him is encapsulated in brief statements known as "Christian doctrines." The Christian community cherishes these doctrines zealously, knowing how important they are for its identity and nurture, and also announces them to the world as truths.

Crucial, plainly, is the relation between *Truth* and *truths*. Clearly *Truth* and *truths* are not the same. The living person of Jesus Christ is categorically different from pronouncements about Him. Nevertheless, He can be embraced as Truth only as the truths about Him are communicated, understood and (through the mysterious ministry of the Holy Spirit) rendered the means whereby He forges Himself within people, forms them as they come to bear His "stamp" and fits them for His service.

11

Doctrines, then, are truths whose importance is determined by the service they render to Truth. Clearly to disregard them is to disregard Him. The Church cannot insist that its Lord is real and at the same cavalierly dismiss doctrine as unimportant, or the amusement of professional theologians or an abstraction that has nothing to do with the solidity of the One who, raised from the dead and thereby established as the Ruler of the cosmos, now "fills all things" (Ephesians 4:10).

As Truth, our Lord is also Way and Life. As Way, He guides us along that path which unfailingly sees us home, having spared us the deadliness of swamp and storm, desert and quicksand. As Life, He quickens our trust in Him and enlivens our obedience to Him. Yet it must always be remembered that He does all of this precisely as we continue to immerse ourselves in the truths that point to Him, speak of Him, and distinguish Him from all other secular and religious "packages" that claim to be a substitute for Him.

Those who are eager to be "doers of the Word" (James 1:22) are frequently impatient with doctrine. To be sure, reading and discussing doctrine is never to be a replacement for "doing" of any sort. Still, it must always be asked how long the Word or Truth will be "done" if truths are trifled with.

Doctrine is needed if each generation is to be instructed in the faith. (From a human perspective, we should remember, the Church is forever a single generation away from extinction.) Doctrine is needed as well if the Church is to fend off the false teaching that is always on the point of infecting it.

And of course doctrine is needed if the Church is to be spared that spiritual and theological "amnesia" wherein it forfeits its identity. We must always recall that in everyday life amnesia, the disappearance of memory, doesn't mean simply that we've

12

forgotten where we've left our umbrella. To be devoid of memory, rather, means that we don't know who we are. Lacking an identity, we can't be trusted. In short, doctrine—truth—is essential if the Church is to continue to know who and what it is; essential if it is to be trusted as witness to the Truth; and essential if it is to continue to be the God-appointed agent of the Saviour's work in the world.

WHAT IS AN EVANGELICAL?

What is an Evangelical? Better, who is an Evangelical? Simply put, Evangelicals are those who glory in the cross of Christ. Our faith arises from it; our thinking converges on it; our life radiates from it.

Evangelicals are aware that the cross has made atonement for all humankind as God made "at one" with Himself disobedient, defiled sinners who were otherwise hopelessly separated from Him by a gaping chasm they were never going to be able to bridge.

Evangelicals know that while God *is* love (1 John 4:8) and can therefore do nothing but love, when God's love encounters human sin his love "burns hot," as Martin Luther liked to say. God's anger or wrath, then, is never the contradiction or denial of his love. (Indifference is always the antithesis of love. After all, the people with whom we are angry we at least take seriously; the people to whom we are indifferent we've already dismissed as insignificant.) God's anger "heats up" only because He loves us so very much and so very relentlessly that He can't remain indifferent to us and won't abandon us. Profoundly He loves sinners more (or at least more truly, more realistically) than we love ourselves, since our self-love, perverted by sin, issues only in self-destruction. And as the cross on which He "did not spare his own Son but gave Him up for us all" (Romans 8:32) makes plain, He longs to spare us torment more than He longs to spare Himself.

We must make no mistake. Because God is holy, sin breaks His heart. More than merely breaking His heart, however, sin also mobilizes His anger and provokes His revulsion. What, then, is God to do with men and women whose ingratitude and insolence have grieved Him, angered Him and disgusted Him? One option is to resign them to what they deserve—except that it's no option at all, since love is all God is. For this reason He sets about recovering and restoring those who were created in His image. Meant to mirror his glory, they now glorify themselves, therein rendering His image unrecognizable.

If the predicament of sinners is to be relieved, then those living in the "far country" (so very far from the Father as to be pronounced "dead, lost" in Luke 15:24) have to be reconciled to Him. Since they are currently in the far country, why don't they just get up and "go home"? There's more to it than this. In point of fact they are where they are not on account of their sin (a misunderstanding heard too often) but on account of God's judgment. Our foreparents, we should recall, didn't cavalierly sashay out of the Garden of Eden or confusedly stumble out or defiantly parade themselves out. They were *driven* out. Who drove them out? God did. He expelled them by a judicious act.

Sin, contrary to much popular thought, does not estrange us from God. Sin mobilizes God's judgment, and God's judgment ensures our alienation from Him. Therefore the invitation to be reconciled to Him can't be issued until His judgment has been dealt with. The cross is that love-fashioned deed of mercy wherein the just Judge absorbs His righteous judgment upon sinners, thereby allowing them to "come home" without in any way "fudging"

His holiness or compromising His integrity or submerging His truth. Only because "in Christ God was reconciling the world to Himself" can the apostle urge, "We beseech you on behalf of Christ, be reconciled to God" (2 Corinthians 5:19-20).

God's tireless pursuit of people who persist in fleeing Him culminates in the cross, wherein He finally overtakes them and wraps them in the arms of the crucified. But of course the cross doesn't appear out of nowhere and insert itself in the year 27 C.E.—it was anticipated through the God-appointed sacrificial system of the Older Testament. For centuries God had been schooling a people, Israel, in the necessity, meaning and ethos of sacrifice, always preparing for the advent of Israel's greater Son.

Reflecting the outlook of the Older Testament, the Newer reflects the priority of the cross on every page. One-half of the written gospels is given over to one week of Jesus' life, the last week wherein His cruciform earthly ministry (John Calvin maintained that the shadow of the cross fell on Jesus' life and ministry from the day He was born) crescendos to the climax of the cross. The first half of the epistles announces the gospel of the cross; the second half unfolds the nature and pattern and rigour of Christian discipleship in the light of the cross. All evangelical understanding, then, emanates from the cross, as do all evangelical faith and obedience.

Evangelicals, then, are those who cherish the "word of the cross," grounded in the atonement, as the "word of truth, the gospel of your salvation" (1 Corinthians 1:18; Ephesians 1:13).

THE PLACE OF PROCLAMATION AND THE NECESSITY OF DECISION

Evangelicals characteristically find themselves constrained to *proclaim* this message because the message is inherently missiological. In other words, the proclamation isn't an "add-on" or an afterthought. Proclamation remains an aspect of the message itself: "gospel" defines itself as "gospel *announced.*" So, far from resembling proselytizing or even propaganda, the proclamation of the gospel belongs to the logic of the gospel. Evangelicals, then, are aware that mission is to God's people as burning is to fire. Burning characterizes fire; apart from burning, fire has no existence. Mission establishes the Church and characterizes it, for God's people are created by the revelation of the cross. We cling to it. We exist for the purpose of announcing a crucified and risen Lord who "fills all things" (Ephesians 1:23; 4:10). Indeed, since Christ "fills" every nook, crevice and corner of the universe, since Christ therefore laps everyone's life at all times, Evangelicals understandably continue to point others to the One whose coming to them spells only blessing.

Such proclamation, needless to say, isn't announced in a "Who cares?" attitude, as if the hearer's response were of no significance, or at least of no *eternal* significance. What's at stake in any announcement of the gospel is always more than a "response" of whim or preference or even prejudice. What's at stake is nothing less than the hearer's salvation. For this reason the declaration of the gospel always elicits a particular decision from the hearer, that "U-turn" which Scripture labels repentance. Such a decision—for which sobriety, solemnity and unrestrained joy are all appropriate simultaneously—is a life-changing "about-face" from darkness to light, from indifference or hostility to love, from death to life. The lattermost point must be given its full weight: the decision to which the gospel summons the hearer has everything on earth and in heaven hanging on it.

Such a decision need not be made in an instant; in fact more often than not it isn't made in an instant. The fact that the process of deciding is protracted in most cases doesn't detract in the slightest from its veracity. Nevertheless, at some point the decision *needs* to have been made as the rebel surrenders, the icy heart is thawed, the spiritually inert is resurrected and Love is loved.

COVENANT FAITHFULNESS AND LIFELONG REPENTANCE

The God who has promised ever to be our God, *God for us*, never rescinds His covenant with us. In turn He longs for us ever to be His people as we own our covenant with Him. Finding us to be covenant-breakers with Him, however, He gives us His Son and directs us to the Nazarene as the one instance of human covenant faithfulness to the Father. For this reason the decision of faith and obedience that we make is not made once only; rather the decision has to be renewed every day. Every morning we must recommit ourselves to our Lord, to His truth, to His way, and—no less, even perhaps hardest of all—to His people. In Luther's famous tract, *The 95 Theses,* which he nailed to door of the Wittenberg church in 1517, the first thesis sets the tone for all that follows. Luther's first thesis will ever remain the "bass note" for all of us: "The Christian life consists of *daily,* lifelong repentance." In other words, every morning we have to reorient ourselves to our Lord, determined to identify ourselves with Him and follow Him *today* amid all dangers, deceptions and distractions.

Yet the decision we make, while it's unquestionably the inception of the Christian life, isn't the termination of that life. Much arduous discipleship lies between commencement and completion. More than a few trials will have to be encountered and temptations resisted. Barnabas and Paul, eager not to misrepresent the rigours of discipleship, are found "strengthening the souls of the disciples, exhorting them to continue in the faith . . . saying that through many tribulations we must enter the kingdom of God" (Acts 14:22). If Evangelicals uphold justification by faith as the beginning of the Christian life and its stable basis, no less ardently do they insist that sanctification, holiness of heart and life, must be pursued at all times and in all circumstances.

HOLINESS

Holiness is simply the believer's conformity to the will and way of the Master. Holiness is God's purpose for His people. While the word-group in Scripture that refers to election or predestination occurs approximately 15 times, the word-group pertaining to holiness occurs 833 times. Plainly the category of holiness dominates Scripture and should therefore be the Christian's preoccupation.

Cherishing the Great Commandment as well as the Great Commission—"You shall love the Lord your God with all your heart, soul, mind and strength" (Mark 12:30) and "Go therefore and make disciples of all nations" (Matthew 28:19)—Evangelicals remain convinced of the "Root" Commandment: "You shall be holy, for I the Lord your God am holy" (Leviticus 19:2). This "root" commandment reverberates like a bell throughout the Bible. Like all commandments, however, the predominant commandment is at the same time the predominant promise: not only *must* God's people be holy; God will see to it that His people *are* holy. God will guarantee for people consecrated to Him everything that He requires of them. Then God's people may and must obey Him in matters great and small as they are conformed to that "holiness without which no one will see the Lord" (Hebrews 14:12).

Such holiness, John Wesley liked to say, pertains to "heart and life." Holiness of heart (i.e., a supposedly grace-wrought disposition) not giving rise to holiness of life is no more than a religious self-indulgence, a pietistic trip "inward" that skeptics rightly see to be rationalized selfism. Holiness of life not grounded in holiness of heart, on the other hand, is no more than self-righteous legalism, and exhausting as well. Holiness of heart and life together attest a simple yet glorious truth that Evangelicals will never surrender: God can do something with sin beyond forgiving it. *What* can He do? Not only can He relieve us of sin's guilt; He can also release us from sin's grip. Deliverance from both the guilt and the power of sin remains a vivid conviction in the evangelical consciousness.

CONSTANT CONVERSION

The decision for faith, then, with concomitant inner and outer holiness, might appear to be an end in itself. In truth it is and it isn't. It's an end in itself in that faith binds us to Jesus Christ, and our union with Him is an end in itself. Any utilitarian consideration or motive here merely attempts to use Him, rendering Him a means to an end, a tool we can exploit for some "goody" apart from Him. *He* is our greatest good, our eternal good. He gives us His unique gifts only in the course of giving us *Himself.* Therefore He can never be a means to anyone's end.

At the same time, the decision for faith invariably binds us not only to Jesus Christ but also to that body of which He is head, namely, the Church. Since believers are bound to Jesus Christ, head and body, we must daily renew our commitment to Christ's people even as we admit with our Puritan ancestors that the Church is a "fair face with an ugly scar." And since in Christ

19

God has "so loved the world" (John 3:16) as never to abandon it, the conversion of which Evangelicals speak must be a daily-renewed conversion to Christ, His people and the world.

KINGDOM OF GOD

To say we must love the world as Christ loves it is to say that we shan't adulate it uncritically or fawn over it or seek to profit from it; rather we shall long for the full manifestation of its redemption. To this end Christians understand that they have been commissioned to render visible that kingdom which Jesus Christ brought with Him in His resurrection from the dead. When we pray "Thy kingdom come" we are praying for the coming manifestation of a kingdom that has to be in our midst just because the King is in our midst. A king without a kingdom is no king at all. Jesus Christ, risen from the dead and present with His people, meets us again and again, not infrequently startling us as He acquaints us with Himself afresh. Since He has promised to abide with us until history is concluded, His kingdom has to have arrived. While it is discerned through the eyes of faith to be sure, it remains invisible to all others.

It follows that one of the Church's tasks is to render indisputable and undeniable that kingdom which is simply the entire creation of God *healed*. Not surprisingly, then, Evangelicals have been at the forefront of the abolition of the slave trade, the amelioration of working conditions in factories and mines, the expansion of literacy, the providing of medical assistance, ministries to the incarcerated, the elevation of women and the relief of human distress of every kind. Believers' holiness of heart and life lends visibility to a world from which Christ's victorious cross has already seen "Satan fall like lightning from heaven," heaven being the invisible dimension of the creation (Luke 10:18).

EVANGELICALISM'S VULNERABILITY

Honesty compels us to admit that evangelicalism is susceptible to distortion and prone to unravel. Rightly emphasizing Christian experience as the gospel "opens the heart" (as happened with Lydia in Acts 16:13), the evangelical consciousness is always in danger of confusing *experience of the Spirit* with *experience-in-general*, especially where experience-in-general is riddled with romanticism or nostalgia or religious sentimentality.

In other words, despite evangelicalism's insistence on *ortho*doxy (*correct* thinking about God and the proper glorifying of Him), evangelicalism remains susceptible to *hetero*doxy (false belief and erroneous glorifying of an other-than-Christ). Evangelical zeal must always be balanced by the tested wisdom of Christians who lived and learned, suffered and witnessed before us. This great weight of Christian wisdom, found in the Church's tradition, is commonly known as "catholicity."

EVANGELICALISM AND CATHOLICITY

Two things are to be noted here. First, the word "catholicity" is spelled with a lower case *c*. An upper case *C* normally refers to *Roman* Catholicism. Roman Catholicism is one denomination within the Christian family. Second, the catholicity of the Church, however, is the accumulated wisdom of Christian memory that is found in all denominations.

Catholicity preserves both identity and universality.[1] Identity is that which distinguishes the Church from the world; universality, that which impels the Church to give itself for

---

1. I am glad to acknowledge my debt to Jaroslav Pelikan, *The Riddle of Roman Catholicism*, and Donald Bloesch, *The Future of Evangelicalism*.

21

the world. Needless to say, only that Church which is self-consciously different from the world can ever exist for the world.

The missionary enterprise of the early Church attests its catholicity. (We should note here that the missionary thrust of the Church isn't the Church's invention, the Church somehow arriving at an insight that the Church's Lord somehow lacked. While Jesus told the Canaanite woman, "I was sent only to the lost sheep of the house of Israel" [Matthew 15:24], unquestionably the seeds of the Gentile mission are found in Jesus' ministry, particularly in His appearances to His followers during the "40 days" between His resurrection and His ascension.) At first Peter opposed this expression of catholicity, Peter maintaining that all Gentile Christians first had to become Jews. Plainly Peter thought that the Church's universality threatened its identity—and he had to be helped to a new perspective.

From a different angle of vision, it's evident that the unique message of the Church guarantees its identity; the assorted converts to the Church guarantee its universality. Both identity and universality have to be held in exquisitely fine balance if the catholicity of the Church is to be preserved. Evangelicals who are properly catholic balance evangelism with training in discipleship and Christian nurture. We balance outreach with worship. We balance contemplation of our reigning Lord and commitment to the world's grief.

Evangelicals who are aware of their catholic heritage balance justification (a new standing before God) and sanctification (a new nature from God); the decision for faith and growth in faith; the call to repentance and the call to sainthood; the Reformation (doctrinal restatement) and revival (the Spirit's flooding over large numbers of people who have not yet welcomed the gospel offer). Evangelicals who know the true meaning of "catholic" embrace both specially endowed leaders and ordered ministry; both spontaneous exclamations of praise and sacramental practice.

In all of this, theologians (including those who amplify the doctrinal statements of such bodies as the Evangelical Fellowship of Canada!) preserve catholicity by *defining* the faith so as to combat heresy arising from within the Church, and also by *defending* the faith so as to combat misinterpretation arising from outside the Church. By defining the faith, theological statements preserve identity; by defending the faith, theological statements preserve universality. The first sentence of the Apostles' Creed exemplifies both. "I believe in God the Father almighty, maker of heaven and earth" plainly speaks of universality; "and in Jesus Christ his only Son our Lord . . . crucified under Pontius Pilate" speaks of identity. Doctrine, adequately articulated, always fulfils both purposes.

THE EVANGELICAL CONSENSUS

For decades now Christians of evangelical persuasion throughout the world have recognized that the seven doctrinal affirmations discussed in the following pages are the foundational "building blocks" of the "faith which was once for all delivered to the saints" (Jude 3). The World Evangelical Fellowship arose in 1950, with representatives from twelve countries. Subsequently renamed the World Evangelical Alliance, the organization now represents 200 million Christians in 123 countries. The following theological statements embody the essential convictions of the WEA and its member organizations internationally.

1

THE HOLY SCRIPTURES

The Holy Scriptures as originally given by God are divinely inspired, infallible, entirely trustworthy, and constitute the only supreme authority in all matters of faith and conduct.

If you want to behold the child," said Martin Luther, "then you must go to the manger." Plainly Luther knew the manger to be the place (the only place) where the Christ child was laid. In his characteristically earthy manner Luther wanted us always to be aware of the crucial relationship between Jesus Christ and the Bible. Only as we immerse ourselves in the book that speaks of Him can we apprehend, cherish and profit from Jesus Christ. At the same time, we shouldn't confuse the book with Him who is Lord of the book. We shouldn't mix up the manger and the One who was found only there—yet forever transcends it.

People become Christians as the crucified One, risen and ascended, steals over them. Thereafter they know that what He has done for them, in them and through them they could never have done for themselves. They are who they are insofar as their Lord has fashioned them His.

This has always been the case. Men and women in the Old Testament were aware that Someone had seized them. The One who continued to act upon them defined Himself in their midst. They called Him "God," knowing that He was not one among many but rather "true God": the sole, sufficient, sovereign, saving One. He stamped Himself upon them, commissioning patriarchs and prophets as His witnesses. Their testimony was plainly the human witness to the God who acts upon His people and simultaneously informs them of the meaning of His acts. Eventually their witness to Him was written down. Scripture appeared.

On one hand Scripture is the human witness to God's saving incursion among us. This point is crucial, for if we undervalue Scripture as human witness then we confuse Scripture with the Lord of Scripture, as if God had collapsed Himself into a book. On the other hand, if Scripture is only a human witness then it has no more than human authority. For this reason God owns and blesses the human witness as His own witness to Himself. In other words, God endorses the testimony of the human witnesses He has appointed. When they write, God "writes" on top of it. To put it differently: unless Scripture is a human witness, we aren't part of God's saving activity. Yet if Scripture is merely human witness, it lacks divine authority.

Scripture, then, isn't the revelation. (Recall: the manger isn't the child.) Nonetheless, the total event of Christ's resurrection is the raising of Jesus from the dead plus the risen One's self-interpretation to the apostles in the course of His appearances to them plus their subsequent writing of all this. Scripture therefore is an aspect of revelation, even a necessary aspect. Holy Scripture, then, is indeed divinely inspired.

Yet we must never think that as Scripture is read God is "culled" from it; nor is God deduced or inferred from it. Scripture attests that *the* characteristic of the living God is that He speaks. When God speaks—whether to Moses and Jeremiah or to Peter and Paul—hearers know who has spoken, and what He has said.

28

The present activity of the living God upon and among and within His people is known as the Holy Spirit. As the Holy Spirit stirs the reader of Scripture and illumines the text of Scripture, God acts afresh. At this point readers aren't acquainted chiefly with what they are reading (the prophetic/apostolic testimony to Jesus Christ); they are now face to face with Jesus Christ Himself in an encounter with Him no less immediate and intense and intimate than Peter's encounter on Easter morning or Paul's encounter years later or that of innumerable people throughout the Church's history.

It's the ministry of the Holy Spirit (i.e., the immediacy, intensity and intimacy of God) that prevents Christians from thinking of Scripture as a sort of Aladdin's lamp: we "rub" it until the "genie" (Jesus Christ) emerges. While we certainly have the Bible in our hands, we never have Christ in our hands. (He has us in His.) We do possess the book; we do not possess Him. He possesses us afresh as He owns our fresh reading of the normative testimony to Him.

Scripture is infallible in that it unfailingly accomplishes that for which it is given. Without fail, as often as it is read, the Father will send the promised Spirit, and the Son will loom before us to seize, save and sustain. Therefore Scripture never fails with respect to its purpose, an ever-renewed encounter with Jesus Christ. For this reason it is entirely trustworthy.

In this encounter, the risen Jesus relieves us of sin's guilt and releases us from sin's grip and sets us on the way that we are to walk with Him. In other words, as surely as He has salvaged us, He claims us as His and insists on an obedience to Him that doesn't hesitate and isn't compromised. Not only does Christ imbue us with that faith by which we are bound to Him, He also claims us for that obedience by which we honour Him.

29

Jesus Christ can't be reduced to the prophets and apostles who speak of Him; nevertheless the form in which Jesus Christ comes to His own is the form of their testimony; i.e., Scripture. Therefore there is no hearing and heeding (believing and obeying) Jesus Christ that doesn't take the form of hearing and heeding Scripture.

Charles Spurgeon maintained that if people are standing around a tiger cage debating the nature and power of the tiger in it, many different arguments will be brought forward even as some people believe them and others don't. Spurgeon maintained that there's one way of persuading people conclusively of the tiger's nature and might: let it out of the cage. It is as Scripture is used in the Church's life and work—"uncaged"—that it will persuade people of its inherent nature and might in the course of persuading them of Christ's.

The whole purpose of the Book of the Lord is to effect our adoring surrender to the Lord of the Book.

2

THE HOLY TRINITY

There is one God, eternally existent in three persons: Father, Son and Holy Spirit.

Sometimes our faces contradicts our hearts. Our hearts may be breaking, and yet we "put on a brave face" for a while to get ourselves to work or so as not to upset our children. No one faults us for this. There are situations, however, where the "disconnect" between face and heart is simply sinful. If we put on a false face in order to exploit others or manipulate them or cloak our cruelty—here the contradiction between face and heart is wicked and renders us forever untrustworthy.

What about God? Are His face and His heart one? Does the "face" He has turned to us in the face of Jesus Christ (2 Corinthians 4:6) disclose His heart or disguise it? The doctrine that God is *eternally* (and therefore *essentially*) triune is the church's recognition that in Him there is neither inadvertent inconsistency between face and heart nor deliberate deception. Because God "eternally exists in three persons" we know that in His dealings with us, God is Himself. Face and heart are one. How can we know this?

The "face" of God came to be known as God drew near to His people and acted among them. As His people reflected on their life-experience under God, their conviction moved from their understanding of His face to their assurance concerning His heart. This is how the Church's understanding of the Trinity arose. (It didn't arise as the mental plaything of underemployed theologians.)

Ancient people thought the world to be riddled with deities who fought among themselves, lied, and could even be bribed. Some deities required hideous expressions of worship such as child sacrifice or sacral prostitution. Then the unforeseeable happened: the One whom we have come to know as *true* God bound a people to Himself and Himself to a people. God acted on behalf of this people, delivering them from slavery and thereafter claiming their loyalty and obedience. He spoke to this people through prophets whom His address had quickened and informed and commissioned. The people came to understand that the "Holy One of Israel" wasn't pre-eminent among many deities but the *only* God. Beside Him there was no other. To suggest anything else was idolatrous.

Centuries later an itinerant preacher from a backwoods town (Nazareth) began a public ministry. Many rabbis did as much. He was a prophet. So was John the Baptist. Jesus differed from them all, however, in that He claimed to speak and act with the authority of God. He forgave sin, knowing (as did His detractors) that only God could do this. He insisted that He had unique access to the mind of the Father. He accepted worship as His right, knowing that the worship of any human is idolatry. He claimed that when human history is concluded He would be its judge—the prerogative of God alone. He made the stunning pronouncement, "I and the Father are one." He didn't "correct" the disciple who cried out to Him, "My Lord and my God."

Was Jesus of Nazareth God or not? Jewish followers who knew that idolatry provoked God as nothing else found themselves constrained to acknowledge Him as "God-with-us" or "Emmanuel."

Their experience of God became even richer. The God who forever remained above them ("transcended" them) even as He had become "God-with-them" now convinced them He was also "God-within-them." "God-within-us" is God in His utmost immediacy, intimacy and intensity: Spirit. They associated dynamic symbols of their Jewish heritage with the Spirit: wind, fire, water. They connected the Spirit with energy, change, effectiveness.

In it all they knew that in His condescension to them and incursion within them God gives not some*thing*, but Himself; always Himself, only Himself. Giver and gift are the same. More than just giver and gift, however, God is the effective act of giving itself. God is giver, gift and giving—simultaneously.

All three are essential. If there were no giver, God would be dead; if a giver but not gift, God would be alive but stingy and indifferent; if giver and gift but not the act of giving, God would be alive and merciful but utterly ineffective.

Giver, gift and giving: these are three aspects of God's singular overflowing kindness and generosity. Ceaseless benevolence is how God *appears* to us, the *face He wears*. Is it who He is in Himself? Christians have always known that the triune face God displays as He relates Himself to us is one with the heart of God Himself. His triune face reflects His eternal triune being: it is God's *essence* to be Father, Son and Holy Spirit. That revelation for which we thank God is always revelation *of* God (the Son) *by* God (the Spirit.) The face of Christ can forever be trusted as the heart of God.

35

The Christian understanding of God as eternally triune protects the Church from the assorted "unitarianisms" that always lap at it.

A unitarianism of the Father (so-called) one-sidedly magnifies the transcendence of God until God is so utterly "high and lifted up" as to be inaccessible—and unknowable, since if God were *only* transcendent, humans couldn't even know this much.

A unitarianism of the Son renders Jesus our palsy-walsy chum. He is the "mate" who supports all our agendas, never challenging us or correcting us. The saccharine sentimentality of this "sweet" Jesus cloys.

A unitarianism of the Spirit uncritically promotes subjectivism, surrendering all appreciation of truth and inflating religious "inwardness" to the point of a frenzy that is as mindless as it is disorderly.

Not to be forgotten in all this is the sobering truth that the God who eternally, essentially exists in three persons doesn't need the creature to love in order to be the God who *is* love (1 John 4:8). If God had created nothing, God would still *be* love, for the Father eternally loves the Son and the Son the Father in the eternal bond of the Spirit. Then Christians should be on their knees in adoring gratitude to the God who admits us to His own life of love. Needing nothing from us, He will yet in His love go to hell and back for us, in order that we might come to love Him—and therein become what He has meant us to be.

3

OUR LORD JESUS CHRIST

Our Lord Jesus Christ is God manifest in the flesh; we affirm His virgin birth, sinless humanity, divine miracles, vicarious and atoning death, bodily resurrection, ascension, ongoing mediatorial work, and personal return in power and glory.

All of us bristle at being deceived. Deception is a particularly irksome kind of dishonesty. Yet the coming of Jesus into the world would have been a deception if God had merely come among us *in the form* of man. Instead the Church confesses that Jesus Christ is God coming among us *as* man. The difference is crucial.

If God were to come in the *form* of man, God would have been masquerading as human without actually being human. The doctrine of the incarnation, on the other hand, states unambiguously that there's no disguise, no duplicity. God hasn't cloaked Himself with our humanity so that He merely *seems* human, as we sometimes cloak ourselves on Halloween to leave acquaintances uncertain who we are.

Rather, God has come among us *as* man precisely to end all guesswork about who He is. Never surrendering His lofty transcendence, He simultaneously assumes our humanity in order to identify Himself with us utterly.

Was that Nazarene man of the *same* nature or substance or essence of the Father, or were the Son and the Father merely *similar*? Everything hangs on the difference.

If Jesus is merely like the Father, the obvious question is "How like? A little bit or a lot?" However similar the Son may be to the Father, if they don't possess the same nature (that is, if Son and Father aren't both *God*), then what the Son does on earth isn't ratified in heaven. While the difference between "run" and "ruin" is the smallest letter of the alphabet, the difference between asking someone to run your business for you and asking her to ruin it is anything but small.

Simply put, the foundation, the building block of the Christian faith is this: Jesus of Nazareth is nothing less than God *as* man.

What if He weren't? Billions of people, after all, insist that He isn't.

If Jesus isn't fully both God and man at the same time then God's love stops short of becoming one with us. If Jesus is only God in the form of man (that is, if God only *seemed* to have become human) then God's love can never be more than apparent, never actually reaching us in our sin, degradation and death. God could never be said to love us unconditionally and limitlessly, for God's love would stop short of His uttermost identification with us.

If Jesus isn't fully both God and man at the same time then His acts aren't the acts of God. Consider Christ's approach to the adulterous woman. Adultery is sin and therefore a violation of God. All sin mobilizes God's anger and disgust. Plainly the woman's predicament is perilous. When Jesus declares her forgiven, is He merely "talking through His hat"—or is she in truth forgiven by the only one who can forgive, namely God? When Jesus declares her forgiven, is she granted the Father's pardon and peace—or is she still facing final condemnation?

Our Lord's declaring her forgiven is frivolous unless His deed and the Father's deed are one.

Jesus' detractors, who correctly define sin as primarily an offence to God (see Psalm 51:4), respond with outrage: "Only God can forgive sin." They are right. Any human who claims to forgive sin is at best a blasphemer and at worst deranged—unless He is God in our midst *as* man.

If Jesus isn't fully both God and man at the same time we remain under condemnation. The cross as a means to end our condemnation seems unjust to many people. Objectors point out that the death of a human who is sinless (Jesus of Nazareth) has no bearing on the judgment of those who are sin-riddled. But they miss the crucial point. While God alone is judge, since the Nazarene is God *as* man, then when God's judgment is deflected onto Jesus, God is absorbing into Himself His own judgment upon humankind.

Atonement occurs as the Just Judge and unholy sinners are made "at one." In other words, it isn't merely a man who suffered and died for us, but *God* as man. It wasn't merely the life of a man that was offered to save us, but *the life of God* as man. For this reason the ancient Church's exclamation is as profound as it is pithy: "Our resurrection is stored up in the cross."

If Jesus isn't fully both God and man at the same time then His "mighty acts" are not the incursion of the kingdom of God but merely pointless, freakish occurrences that remain forever unrelated to both a promised kingdom and our human existence. Since Jesus of Nazareth is God *as* man, however, our Lord's miracles are signs of the breaking-in of the Kingdom— moreover, they *are* that kingdom now operative in our midst. They are instances of a kingdom "that cannot be shaken" (Hebrews 12:28), nothing less than the creation of God healed.

Since humankind cannot invent the incarnation (who besides God could ever fashion God in our midst *as* man?); since humankind cannot generate its saviour (what can sinners produce besides sinners?); since history cannot give rise to its own redeemer (what can history yield besides a glaring need for redemption?)—then the virgin birth of our Lord singularly testifies to the truth that the Incarnate One, Saviour and Redeemer, has to be *given* to us in a unique act of God.

Those whom the Spirit has quickened recognize this unarguable truth: what all human existence and human history need, God Himself must provide, since sinners immersed in a history of sin cannot fashion their own cure.

In the same way Christ's bodily resurrection is essential if our inescapably bodily existence is to be restored to its integrity—essential, indeed, if all the contradictions of the creation's earthiness are to be canceled and the creation is to stand forth whole once again.

Needless to say, the Incarnate One whose effectual ministry in the days of His flesh was book-ended by virgin birth and bodily resurrection—this One is now neither lost to us nor "out to lunch." Ascended, He intercedes for His "friends" (Hebrews 7:25; John 15:9) as He did throughout His earthly ministry.

Admittedly, anyone at all may dispute everything that's been said concerning "God manifest in the flesh." The day has been appointed, however, when the truth of the Nazarene will be beyond dispute as God's way with us is vindicated and the incarnation redounds to the praise and glory of Him who does all things well (Mark 7:24).

4

SALVATION BY FAITH

The salvation of lost and sinful humanity is possible only through the merits of the shed blood of the Lord Jesus Christ, received by faith apart from works, and is characterized by regeneration by the Holy Spirit.

U nless you are born anew, you cannot see the kingdom of God, Jesus insists to Nicodemus (John 3:3). If we can't even *see* the kingdom apart from new birth, how much less are we able to *enter* it? It's no wonder that John Calvin spoke of regeneration as "the most important thing in the kingdom of God."

Nicodemus, however, is puzzled. For how can an adult reappear in his mother's uterus? He has misinterpreted the Greek word *anothen*. It can mean "again" in the sense of "one more time, a chronological repetition"; or "from above (that is, at the hand of God)"; or "remade without blemish or imperfection." Nicodemus fastens on the first meaning only; Jesus has in mind the latter two only.

Our Lord knows that a fresh start in life is pointless if the new beginning merely reproduces the "old" man or woman corrupted by the same sin. He maintains, rather, that everyone needs a qualitatively new existence, and this can come only "from above," as a gift of God.

While the word *anothen* occurs only once in Scripture, the truth it embodies is found everywhere. Paul speaks repeatedly of "new creation" and "new man/woman" and "newness of life." Peter speaks of Christians as "newborn babes." Jesus warns against causing "little ones" to stumble, spiritually newborn people of any chronological age.

Centuries earlier the prophet Ezekiel heard God promise a new heart of flesh, unlike the old heart of stone. Whereas the old was inert and insensitive, the "new heart and new spirit" (Ezekiel 18:31) would throb, alive unto God.

Plainly the alternative to new birth is old death, eternal death. In Christ's well-known parable, that of the two sons, the father's joy overflows at his estranged son's reconciliation and return from the far country. Why? Just because this son of mine "was dead and is alive again; he was lost and is found."

"Dead." "Lost." This is the spiritual predicament of fallen men and women. It is grim. Lost to whom? Lost eternally before God. We must never reduce the gospel to a form of existentialist philosophy wherein salvation is merely rescue from being lost to oneself (people aren't sure who they are) or from being lost concerning life's purpose (they find life meaningless).

"Lost, dead" refers rather to our predicament before God. To be "dead in trespasses and sins" (Ephesians 2:1) is to be lost *ultimately.*

At the same time, since the creature has no rights or power over the Creator, we should never think that spiritual death is something we have brought upon ourselves. Death is God's judgment upon our rebellious disobedience and our insolent ingratitude. Adam and Eve didn't flee the garden of Eden: God's judicial act *drove* them out. It expelled them and barred any attempt they might make to regain it.

Since God's judgment has driven them away, only God's judgment *rescinded* can re-admit them and reconcile them to

Him. Apart from a divine act of incomprehensible mercy, the fate of humankind—"dead, lost"—is sealed. This is the reason the cross leaves all believers breathless: in the cross God acted mercifully to reconcile and regenerate those whose predicament is otherwise hopeless.

The sacrifice of God's Son fulfils the sacrifices Israel offered for centuries. The purpose of Israel's sacrifices was to allow sin-defiled people to approach the holy God without thereby being annihilated, as well as to render them holy in turn. Blood gathered from sacrificial victims and poured upon the altar— even poured upon worshipers—would issue in sins forgiven and hearts renewed, as Ezekiel promised.

The Day of Atonement saw two goats offered up as part of the divinely ordained prefiguration of the cross (Leviticus 16:8-15). One goat was sacrificed in the sanctuary and its blood sprinkled on the mercy-seat, where the Holy and the defiled meet. The second was driven into the wilderness, having had Israel's sin confessed over it and laid upon it. The first sacrifice averted God's wrath; the second bore away Israel's sin.

Both sacrifices are gathered up in the cross. The New Testament speaks of the first as "propitiation" and the second as "expiation." Propitiation averts God's anger (always at God's initiative), thus making it possible for the sinner to hear and heed the invitation to "come home." Expiation makes it possible for the sinner to come home guilt-free.

Apostolic testimony characteristically sounds both truths. Christ's blood has "saved [us] from the wrath of God" (Romans 5:9). At the same time the crucified one "bore our sins in his body on the tree" (1 Peter 2:24). The singular act of the cross both satisfies the Father's judgment and bleaches our stain.

Still, all that the Saviour has accomplished for us and now longs to effect in us by the power of the Spirit comes to be ours only as we own Him in faith. Spirit-wrought faith is the bond whereby we are united to Him. We are made beneficiaries of His sacrifice and henceforth identified as new creatures.

Why is it all to be "received by faith apart from works"? The answer is simple: our "works" are our attempts at self-acquittal and self-renewal. Our works indicate that we foolishly prefer to trust our self-righteousness (no righteousness at all) instead of abandoning ourselves to the righteousness God has fashioned for us in the cross. Such attempts amount to monumental ingratitude and blind folly.

Since such attempts are themselves sin-riddled, they are patently ridiculous. Any putting forward of our own "works" is undeniably our effort at contributing to our salvation, wherein we would claim some credit. Faith, on the other hand, is our commitment to the Saviour who is Himself our salvation.

Contribution (of works) and commitment (of faith) are mutually exclusive and jointly exhaustive. Either we cling to whatever it is we want to thrust before God as a bargaining chip or we open our hand, drop what we had thought to impress Him, and seize in faith the provision He has fashioned for us. There is no other possibility.

For this reason the hymn writer had it right when he wrote, "*Nothing* in my hand I bring; simply to thy cross I cling."

5

THE HOLY SPIRIT

*The Holy Spirit enables believers to live a holy life,
to witness and work for the Lord Jesus Christ.*

M any people are quick to understand what is meant by "Father" or "Son" (i.e., Jesus Christ) yet seem uncomprehending when they hear "Holy Spirit." In the earliest Christian congregations, however, the Spirit was identified with startlingly vivid *experience*. Paul asks one group, "Did you receive the Spirit through works of the law or through hearing with faith?" (Galatians 3:2). It's as though he said, "That raging headache you have now: did you get it from having a brick fall on your head or from drinking ultra-cold ice water?" The one matter that is undeniable is the headache. In other words, the apostle was appealing to their *experience* of the Spirit and asking them to recall the means (believing the gospel) by which a reality had seized them that was as undeniable as it was glorious.

The experience of early Christians was nothing less than astonishing. The Spirit had brought the gospel to them "not only in word . . . but also in *power* and with *full conviction*" (1 Thessalonians 1:5). The Spirit had suffused them with joy when, harassed and discriminated against, there was no earthly reason for their rejoicing.

51

Week after week at their worship the Spirit vivified the preaching and rendered it the vehicle of Christ's seizing them afresh. The Spirit inspired their worship, making their praise lively and life-giving. The Spirit collapsed walls within congregational life so that hostile stand-offs gave way to genuine fellowship.

The Spirit was the power by which they were fortified to resist—and more than resist, oppose by exemplifying something better—the lurid blandishments of a social environment whose sex ethic bore no resemblance to the command and claim of the Holy God. (The church in Corinth, it must be remembered, existed in a seaport that was as notorious for its sex trade as are certain cities in Southeast Asia today.)

"Spirit" is the English translation of "pneuma," the Greek word meaning "wind," "breath" or "air." A pneumatic drill has power enough to crack reinforced concrete, overcoming all resistance. At the same time, the highest-speed dental drills, air-driven, facilitate ultra-delicate surgery even as they relieve pain and promote health. A car with an airless tire goes nowhere, and any animated creature without breath is dead. Everywhere in Scripture, pneuma is associated with power and life.

Yet the risen, ruling Lord Jesus Christ pours forth the *Holy* Spirit in order that His people—alive, alert, active in His name— might be rendered holy inwardly and display it outwardly. Such holiness must never be confused with religious knowledge. While the Hebrew word for "holy" means "separate" or "different," the difference the Holy Spirit makes isn't trivial. It has to do, rather, with what lies at the root or foundation of life.

Indeed, the "Root Commandment" of Scripture is God's command in Leviticus 19:2, "You shall be holy, for I the Lord your God am holy." In fact Scripture is so preoccupied with holiness, both God's and ours, that variations of this commandment appear on virtually every page. God is clearly consumed with reaffirming His own holiness in the wake of sinners having denied it, and re-establishing our holiness in the wake of sinners having turned away from it.

The purpose of the cross, the centrepoint of Scripture, isn't that we should be forgiven—it's that we should be rendered holy, forgiveness being the first step toward our holiness. Obviously nothing is more important than the recovery of our holiness, not least because without it we shall not "see the Lord" (Hebrews 12:14). In other words, Spirit-wrought holiness is *the* qualification for our ultimate blessedness, our apprehension of God in which we find ourselves "lost in wonder, love and praise," to quote an old hymn.

If we are going to be "lost" in this sense, we must first become "lost" in a different sense now: the world must be crucified to us as we are crucified to the world (Galatians 6:14). In other words, the Holy Spirit empowers Christ's people for holy living as there ceases to be anything in us that a fallen world can exploit and there ceases to be anything in a fallen world that we crave. Holiness means that we can't be co-opted by sin's agenda and we don't long for what sin offers.

At this point holiness is synonymous with freedom. Christ's people, being made holy through the power of the Spirit, are being freed from all that inhibits their full-flowering as children of God and at the same time are being freed for their vocation as servants of the Master Himself. Now there springs forth from them transparent love, uncontrived joy, peace, patience, kindness, "gentle strength" (meekness) and self-control. Freed from the clutches of their depraved self, Christ's people cease to live in themselves and live elsewhere—specifically, "in" two others: in Christ by faith, and in their neighbours through love as they assist the needy, suffer with the pained and share the shame of the disgraced (to paraphrase Martin Luther).

Yet the Holy Spirit renders God's people holy not merely as an end in itself. The Spirit moves us to witness, vivifies our witness and guarantees its efficacy. To be sure, witness is always the responsibility of the Church. (In Acts, no one comes to faith in Jesus Christ apart from the community's witness.) At the same time, only the Holy Spirit renders such witness effective. Testimony is our responsibility; success is God's.

Whenever the Church forgets this (usually because we find the Spirit moving too slowly), it attempts to engineer the success of its own mission. The result is counter-productive, since the Church, in its impatience, coerces people psychologically or even physically. When it coerces, the Church advertises its unbelief, since it plainly doesn't trust God to do what God alone can.

Genuinely to believe in the Holy Spirit, however, is to pursue our responsibility concerning witness while trusting God to honour His.

It is much the same with the Kingdom-work that Christians undertake. We must work as if everything depended on us, and pray as if everything depended on the Spirit. In fact there's no "as if" about it. Everything *does* depend on us even as all effectiveness, all kingdom-success, depends on the Spirit alone.

6

THE CHURCH AS CHRIST'S BODY

The Church, the body of Christ, consists of all true believers.

Even as the New Testament mentions 188 ways of speaking of the Church (some of the more common ones being salt, light, temple, bride and building), the chief analogy is body. Christians are the body of Christ.

Obviously we can have a relationship with Jesus Christ only as we are related to His body. No one can glory in the head of the body while disdaining the body itself. No one can cherish Jesus Christ while disdaining His people, love Him while despising His "hands and feet" in the world.

Just as we can have a relationship with Jesus only as we are members of His body, in the same way we can have a public identity as Christians only as we are publicly identified with the Church. The only suitable answer to the question "Are you a Christian?" is this: "Yes, I embrace Jesus Christ in faith *and I embrace His people in love.*"

We should always be aware that individually we can be useful in the service of our Lord only as we are members of His body. Rather crudely, the apostle asks us to think of a normal human body and then to imagine a leg detached from it "over there," an arm somewhere else—the sort of ghastly dismemberment we might see at the site of an accident.

"Now," he asks, "of what use is a detached leg?" Plainly, no use at all. Not only is a detached leg useless, can it even be said to be a leg? If a leg is defined as that which supports and propels a torso, then a detached "leg" isn't a leg at all.

The purpose of an eyeball is to see. Then is a detached eyeball, unable to see because detached from nerve and brain, an eye at all?

Once any body member becomes detached it's no more than a piece of decomposing flesh—unsightly, malodorous and above all, useless.

The Church is no collection of independent parts. Rather, it is the family or society into which believers are unavoidably born again. As one of the chief foreparents of Protestant evangelicalism put it: "There is no other way to enter into [Christian] life unless this mother conceive us in her womb, give us birth, nourish us at her breast, and lastly, unless she keeps us under her care and guidance until, putting off mortal flesh, we become like the angels. Our weakness does not allow us to be dismissed from her school until we have been pupils all our lives" (that's John Calvin, in his *Institutes* 4.1.4).

This truth is one Christians have characteristically agreed on: faith in Jesus Christ isn't quickened and cannot thrive apart from the Church. The Church's nurture and protection, instruction and edification will be needed until the day when faith gives way to sight and Christ's people are beyond the reach of seduction, distraction and sloth. The Church is essential to God's economy of salvation.

"But surely," someone objects, "when you speak of Christ's body you don't mean the local congregation; you don't mean St. Matthew's-by-the-Shopping-Mall. Why, in that congregation there are all kinds of problems and more than a few power plays." (It has been said—truly—that the church is like Noah's Ark: if it weren't for the storm outside no one could stand the stink inside.) "Surely *that* congregation isn't the body of Christ."

Yes, it is. Our Lord's body may be scarred, marred, pock-marked, even deformed or crippled in some respect. Nevertheless, it's the only body He has.

When Christians in Corinth were ripping apart their fellowship through their bickering, party spirit and out-and-out wickedness, Paul asked them sharply, "Do you despise the Church?" (1 Corinthians 11:22). That stopped them in their tracks. They knew what he was going to say next: "If you do, then you visit contempt upon your Saviour, and you can't be Christians at all." Yet the apostle never doubted the authenticity of their faith—they clung to and exulted in their risen Lord—even as he knew that God alone searches the heart and therefore God alone must be allowed to distinguish ultimately between true believers and mere formalists.

The passage from Calvin also makes another useful point. Since Father and mother together "parent" believers, Christ's people must "believe the Church" without ever believing *in* the Church. To believe *in* it would be to confuse the fellowship of Christ's people with the Lord of that fellowship—a confusion amounting to idolatry. While the Church alone is entrusted with the gospel, the Church never mutates into the gospel.

In short, the twin pitfalls that have haunted Church history—confusing the Church with its Lord or else severing the Church from its Lord—have to be avoided at all times.

In everyday life the function of our body is to do what our head tells it to do. What the head wills the body to do is transmitted through our nervous system, since nerves connect mind and muscle. Jesus Christ has a body on earth (His muscles, as it were) in order that His will for humankind be done. Christ's purpose for His human (and non-human) creation will be accomplished only as there's a body that receives the directives from the head, recognizes them and implements them. In turn the body's proper functioning pleases Christ its head, and the delight head and body find in each other advances Christ's mission and encourages His people.

There's at least one thing more we should be reminded of when reflecting on the Church as the body of Christ: the body will last as long as the head lasts. This truth can be a great comfort when people suggest the Church is at risk. To be sure, any one congregation or denomination may be at risk (all we need do is recall how many have disappeared), but Christ's body is no more at risk than Christ Himself is, and He is never at risk. He has been raised victor over death. He has been enthroned at the right hand of the Father. The powers of destruction cannot prevail against Him; that is, cannot prevail against *head and body alike.*

The body of Christ existed long before we were added to it. It will thrive long after we have moved from the Church militant to the Church triumphant. The community of Christ's people will never disappear. The Church is weak? God will strengthen it. Confused? God will enlighten it. Corrupt? God will purify it. "I shall build my church," says Jesus, "and the powers of destruction shall not prevail against it" (Matthew 16:18).

THE DAY OF JUDGMENT

*Ultimately God will judge the living and the dead,
those who are saved unto the resurrection of life, those
who are lost unto the resurrection of damnation.*

Justification by faith means that the Day of judgment has been brought from the future to the present, and believers who are now declared rightly related to God are by that fact pronounced "Not guilty. Acquitted." Judgment can hold no terrors for them. "Fearing" God in this life, they will never have to be afraid of Him, even in the life to come.

Their approaching biological cessation is but the slightest interruption, a momentary inconvenience, in a journey that began with their new birth and will conclude with their admittance to the "great cloud of witnesses," God's people who have remained faithful amidst discouragement and fatigue and are now engulfed in long-awaited splendour.

While God's people certainly await heaven, they have already begun to experience it. The apostle Paul speaks of the Spirit, God Himself in His utmost immediate and intense and intimate presence within believers, as the "guarantee" of their safe arrival in the Sabbath rest He has promised His people.

"Guarantee" translates the Greek word *arrabon*, a term in the ancient world used in everyday commerce to speak of "down payment" or "first instalment." Purchasers made a "down payment" on an article so dear to them that they had to have it, the first instalment pledging the payment of many more. In modern Greek *arrabon* is a woman's engagement ring. Deliriously happy as she is now in the love that soaks her, she eagerly anticipates a richer, more intimate and therefore more intense experience of her beloved on the day that she marries.

Christians are aware of the Spirit as God's incursion whereby they are constrained to confess "Jesus is Lord!" The Spirit moves them to cry spontaneously "Abba! Father!" as they are made God's children and are brought into His family. The Spirit brings forth characteristic "fruits" that render Christ's people unmistakable and undeniable, a city set on a hill. Plainly the Spirit is guarantee in the sense that current experience of their Lord assures Christians of a future that is as indescribable as it is indubitable.

Yet Scripture never suggests that heaven is the destiny of all humankind just because God created us all. Solemnly Jesus identified the fork in the road on every day of His public ministry. There are two gates, one leading to destruction and the other to life. While two masters beckon, only one can be served. Treasures can be laid up either on earth or in heaven, the venue of one's investment determining the nature of one's heart (and one's future).

Soberly Jesus insisted every day that repentance, that "U-turn" which the gospel urges all to make, shouldn't be put off. The theme of final judgment is found in virtually all His parables. "The Two Sons" (also known as "The Prodigal Son") tersely insists that the son "in the far country" is "lost, dead"—a spiritual condition that the final judgment doesn't confer but merely confirms. Jesus' Hebrew name "Ye-hosuha" means "God saves," for He has been appointed Saviour—even as His mother is told "this child is set for the fall and rising of many in Israel."

No apostle thinks differently. Paul warns spiritual dilettantes about the coming wrath. Peter tells readers that God is neither slow nor sleepy concerning His promise to conclude human history; God is simply prolonging the day of grace and protracting opportunity for repentance. John maintains that Christ came not in order to condemn but in order to save; still, to disdain the proffered salvation is to be left with condemnation. James warns careless people that the Judge is standing at the door. Jude laments that some are "devoid of the Spirit," a vacuity so significant that to be devoid of the Spirit is ultimately to lack everything.

Since God *is* love—love is all there is to God—then final, irretrievable spiritual loss points up the enormity of sin. Surrounded by blessing only, the impenitent repudiate it only to find curse. Similarly, ultimate loss points up the monstrosity of sin, as those who are the beneficiaries of God's infinite goodness maliciously throw it all back in His face. And of course condemnation highlights sin's irrationality, its sheer incomprehensibility: why would anyone facing eternal loss persist in spurning God's provision and sneering at God's mercy, and do all of this in a flaunted posture of insolence and ingratitude?

To be sure, there has never been a lack of "universalists" who maintain that all will be saved inasmuch as all are saved now, thanks to the event of the cross; or who maintain that all will be saved eventually inasmuch as no one will finally be able to hold out against a love whose winsomeness will prove irresistible.

Scripture, however, supports neither position. While the cross has made atonement *for* sinners, reconciliation and righteousness become effective only *in* sinners who give up their headlong flight past the arms of the crucified and instead embrace the

One whose outstretched arms have already embraced them. Assuredly the cross is God's publicly announced declaration of amnesty with sinners. They, however, must in turn confess their amnesty with Him.

Is it true, then, that in the end the Sovereign God can be defied by a mere creature, albeit disobedient? Unlike humans who mistake sovereignty for control or coercion, God so respects the integrity of the creature made in His image that He will not violate it. God honours to the end the integrity of persons made to reflect *the* Person, never treating as a thing or object the one creature who is always a subject or agent. God remains unassailable: the unbeliever's rejection of Him threatens neither His security nor His identity.

Then do believers face no judgment at all? Let's be clear: they face no condemnation, although even the holiest must be confronted with the arrears of sin that remain in them. Impurities will have to be removed if they are to appear "without spot or blemish." Yet none of this can overturn the "good and faithful servant" pronouncement God speaks to them, even as nothing can eclipse their sight of Him whom they have known by faith and now behold face to face.

THE FUNCTION OF
DOCTRINE

I n the preceding chapters we have explored seven doctrinal statements that Evangelicals consider to be essential to Christian belief. This naturally leads us to the question of practical application: What is the proper function of doctrinal statements in the Church's life?

Before answering that question we should first note that *doctrinal standards are inevitable.* The human mind naturally seeks to order what it knows.[2] We are never content merely with apprehending truths. Invariably we want to apprehend them in their relationship to each other and to apprehend them in their integration as a whole. In other words, we want to grasp the "total picture" that cogent, coherent truths yield.

With respect to the relationship of doctrinal truths to each other, it's important for us to be clear on the difference between "internal" and "external" relationships. If items are related to each other externally, then removing one doesn't alter those that remain. Removing one sugar cube from a box full of sugar

---

2. William Abraham's *Waking from Doctrinal Amnesia* (Nashville: Abingdon Press, 1995) has stimulated my thinking with respect to the place of doctrine in the Church's life.

cubes, for instance, in no way alters the nature of the sugar cubes that remain. Things are internally related, on the other hand, if removing one alters another. If I, a married man, suffer the loss of my wife, then I am no longer husband, regardless of how else I might be described.

To say that doctrines are internally related is to acknowledge that if, for instance, the doctrine of the Incarnation is denied (or merely overlooked, since Christians, congregations and denominations are much more prone to lose sight of something crucial on account of neglect or distraction or fad-chasing than they are to repudiate doctrine formally), then the doctrine of the Holy Spirit ("pneumatology") is distorted so thoroughly as to be denatured. For the Holy Spirit without the Incarnation isn't the power that the risen Lord Jesus bears and bestows, but is rather a non-specific power unrelated to the saving purposes of the Son. It (plainly the Spirit is no longer *He*) will readily be claimed to legitimate any cause at all, and will as readily be co-opted to fuel and feed any human undertaking, however unconnected to the Kingdom. Saddest of all, perhaps, when the doctrines of Son and Holy Spirit are no longer understood to be internally related, any thoughtful Christian who is dubious of what's now claimed to be God-inspired is accused of spiritual insensitivity or even Spirit-resistance.

In the same way, if the doctrines of Creation and Redemption aren't understood to be internally related, then Creation, no longer needing to be restored by a specific *act* of God—who can act upon the creation salvifically only if he is utterly distinct from the creation—will come to be viewed as an emanation of God or an extension of God or an aspect of God. Isn't this exactly what has happened with the New Age Movement, with its age-old heresy of pantheism or pan*en*theism (i.e., God is either the essence of all that is or God is *in* the essence of all that is)? If Redemption isn't seen to be *necessarily* related to Creation, then the Kingdom of God is never seen to be the whole creation *healed*, and redemption is reduced to a "fix-me-up" for religious individuals who have long since abandoned that world which God so loves as never to forsake.

Since confusion is never God-honouring, humans are constrained to recognize and acknowledge the inherent order and integration of all that they have come to know. The conviction that arises as ordered, integrated truth grips us is a conviction rendered firmer, deeper and more comprehensive as the compactness, weightiness and consistency of truth forges itself upon us ever more profoundly. Where order and integration are lacking, people regard themselves not as helped by the inundation of truths but rather overwhelmed, for now they feel themselves bombarded by a welter that only leaves them perplexed, weary and prone to fragmentation. In other words, truth's cogency and consistency are essential if we are to know whose we are and therefore who we are. To know who we are as God's people means that doctrine must be grasped as a whole and its constituent parts seen in their internal inter-relatedness.

Faith thinks, and must think. God is never honoured through unnecessary ignorance or intellectual indolence or thoughtlessness or irrationality. In other words, we cannot claim to know and love Jesus Christ while remaining cavalier about or indifferent to the doctrines that describe Him and allow us to commend Him to others.

DOCTRINE AND SELF-DEFINITION

The Church needs doctrine too in its engagement with the world around it. As the gospel impels the Church to engage the world, the Church ought to be clear as to what the "world" is. The world isn't the cosmos—i.e., the vast expanse of the universe; according to the Gospel of John, rather, the world is the sum total of disobedient men and women who have "packed" on God (in the way a class can "pack" on a teacher) in their hostility to Him who is their only hope. Christians who fail to understand the "world" in this way will be dumbfounded at the world's deafness concerning the gospel, immobilized soon by discouragement at the world's recalcitrance and eventually victimized by those whom Christians endeavour to help. In short, doctrinal naïveté renders them clueless, defenceless and useless.

At all times we must speak with such clarity as to forestall all ambiguity concerning who we are and what we are about—and this not only to ourselves but also to those who have not yet joined us. In other words, those who confess the faith must understand what they are upholding, while those who disavow it should understand precisely what it is they've said they are rejecting. Think of the expression that gathers up the whole of the Christian life in the Apostles' Creed: "I believe in the forgiveness of sins." Every word in this expression is freighted with gospel meanings; without the doctrines that articulate the gospel those inside the Church as well as those outside can only remain unaware of what is being upheld and what is being jettisoned.

Who, for instance, is the "I" who believes? Is it the "I" of Descartes' "I think, therefore I am"? In other words, is the human being *defined* by the capacity to think self-reflectively? Or is "I" the subject of feeling, as Romanticism tells us? Aristotle maintained that the human being is a rational animal. We differ from the animals in that we can do algebra. Several matters clamour for our attention at this point. Is the defining difference between us and the ape merely the fact that we can perform intellectual operations of greater complexity? Apart from doctrine, no one can be expected to know that while God made animals and humans on the same "day," and while God loves and protects the animals no less than He does us, humans are the only creatures to whom God speaks and from whom He expects a response. Since God speaks to us, we are response-*able* and therefore response-*ible*. And as for rationality, haven't figures such as Marx, Freud and Foucault shown repeatedly that 90 percent of what we call reasoning is actually rationalization whereby we unconsciously attempt to legitimize our aspiration to social climbing (Marx) or live with our inadmissible psycho-sexual conflicts (Freud) or defend the mindset of our peers who are also privileged to have their hands on the levers of social power (Foucault)?

And what about forgiveness? Most people persist in confusing forgiving with excusing, such as when they say, "I can forgive you, since there are circumstances that excuse what you have done to me." Only adequate doctrine allows us to understand that what is excusable is to be excused; what is *utterly inexcusable* can only be *forgiven*. When we are excused, then, we are not being judged; but when we are forgiven (by God or our fellows) judgment has most certainly been visited upon us. Only the guilty, after all, need to be forgiven.

Needless to say, "sin" is prone to the same misunderstandings. Most people confuse sin and immorality. Lacking the gospel and the doctrine that speaks of it, they don't get the point that's evident every day in the earthly ministry of Jesus: the moral person is sinner no less than the immoral, and the moral person sins as much in her morality as the immoral person in her immorality. (Paul says that Jesus died for the "ungodly" not the immoral, "ungodly" comprehending moral and immoral alike.)

The force of many of our Lord's parables is that the moral are no closer to the Kingdom than those they despise.

"Believe," of course, is vulnerable to the same distortion wherever doctrine is disregarded. To "believe," biblically, isn't to add one or several items to one's mental storehouse, as if to believe were primarily a cerebral matter. To believe, rather, is to *abandon* ourselves to the Lord who has already given himself to us without hesitation, qualification or reservation.

THE PASTORAL NEED FOR DOCTRINE

There will always be a pastoral need for doctrine. Doctrine may be likened to a recipe or a roadmap. Just as a recipe isn't the meal to be eaten nor a roadmap the terrain to be traversed on the way to one's destination, apart from the recipe the meal might turn out to be inedible if not toxic; and apart from the roadmap we shall surely fail to find our way across the terrain and thereby forfeit safe arrival at our destination. Only with the help of doctrine will we "taste and see that the Lord is good" (Psalm 34:8).

There are many pastoral endeavours that always require "recipe" and "roadmap." Think of preaching. Preaching, a human undertaking to be sure, bears no little resemblance to other human undertakings, such as the speech-arts. Preaching may borrow judiciously from communications-theory and practice, from rhetoric (the art of persuading), from dialectic (the art of refuting), from the theatrical. Yet the activity of preaching is none of these exactly. The doctrine of preaching is essential if preaching is to remain true to its divine mandate and help hearers "taste and see." And what is this doctrine? – the offering of the Incarnate Word by means of a spoken word that is formed, informed and normed by the Written Word.

74

In all of this preaching (undeniably a human activity and human event) becomes, by God's grace, a divine event as the risen crucified one *Himself* now surges over the hearer and fosters in the hearer both the desire to heed Him and the capacity to do so. For this reason John Calvin liked to say that when the sermon is preached, the blood of Jesus drips on the congregation. No expert in communications-theory will ever come to close to grasping how the preaching of the gospel is related to the action of the ascended Son as the latter looms before the worshipper and constrains the worshipper to recommitment and reconsecration.

In the same way missiology, apart from doctrine, will become ever more dilute as secularization proceeds, ending up as merely yet another instance of cross-cultural communication. Pastoral care will become indistinguishable from the dispensation of humanistic wisdom and indistinguishable as well from any and all kinds of community-formation, the Church becoming merely one more sodality consisting of those who gather themselves around a common interest or activity. Spiritual direction, a huge item today in the formation of candidates for the ordained ministry and a growing concern among the laity as well, is always in danger of becoming amateurish psychotherapy or counselling that happens (coincidentally) to employ a religious vocabulary.

Admittedly, doctrine (a statement) is categorically different from Jesus Christ (a person). Nonetheless, in the course of all that happens in Church life, only doctrine will keep us using Christian language that possesses Christian content since doctrine continues to orient our understanding to the living person of Jesus Christ. Apart from doctrine, words like "grace," "love," "faith," "hope" and "sin" will detach themselves from

Him, ultimately surrendering all connection with the Truth that Jesus is, inasmuch as they have surrendered all connection with the truths that speak of Him.

DOCTRINE AND EVANGELISM

Most tellingly, the Church's mandate concerning evangelism impels the Church to cherish doctrine. To evangelize is to commend the world's sole, sufficient Sovereign and Saviour to those who have not yet heard or at least not yet responded. Why is it important that people hear and respond? There is only one adequate reason: people are disobedient, defiant, disdainful sinners, and the Day has been appointed when they must appear before the One whose judgment cannot be deflected or denied. While the *human situation* changes from era to era (there are challenges, for instance, in the era of genetic splicing and nuclear weaponry that were unknown in earlier eras), the *human condition* never changes. The human condition, in the wake of the Fall (a disaster that only doctrine, it should be noted, can describe) can be spoken of briefly and bluntly: having denied God's holiness and having contradicted their own, sinners now live before the Just Judge who, in his astounding mercy, has made provision for them. It is impossible to speak of the human condition, the possibility of ultimate loss, the economy of salvation, the nature of repentance and faith, the blandishments of the evil one, the nurture of the Church and the appointment to glory; without doctrine it is impossible to speak here to those whose predicament is nothing less than perilous.

When doctrine is allowed to recede, evangelism becomes a chatty forum or an exercise in group dynamics or the application of techniques for institutional growth. Evangelism that denies what's at stake for the hearer—*everything* eternal and temporal—

is simply evangelism that has reduced itself to psychology: hearers' responses may make a difference to how they feel but settle nothing of eternal consequence. If ultimate loss isn't possible, then neither is anything or anyone at risk at any time, and evangelism doesn't proffer what is to be found nowhere else—and isn't needed in any case.

Doctrine will be necessary if "I believe in Jesus Christ" is to retain its inherent substance, integrity and efficacy.

HOW DO DOCTRINAL STANDARDS FUNCTION?

(1) Doctrinal standards provide a means whereby "the faith which was once for all delivered to the saints" (Jude 3) is in turn delivered from generation to generation. We are not the first generation of Christians. Neither does it appear we are going to be the last. If the present generation, the previous ones and those to follow are all alike to be defined as "Christian," then there has to be a means whereby the one word genuinely applies to all and applies inasmuch as the one reality is cherished by all. Doctrinal standards facilitate both. To uphold doctrine is to "guard the truth that has been entrusted to you" (2 Timothy 1:14).

(2) Doctrinal standards provide a "first line of defence" against false teaching. Scripture gives much space to the repudiation of false teaching. The Older Testament is always concerned to help God's people identify and reject false prophets. Much of the Newer Testament is written on account of the need to safeguard Christians against false teaching. The church in Corinth had come to think that since we are saved by grace through faith on account of Christ, how we behave thereafter doesn't matter, while the church in Galatia erred in the opposite direction: how we behave is what finally saves us. The second epistle of Peter,

along with the epistle of Jude, explicitly warns Christians about the pernicious consequences of embracing the message of false teachers who have managed to infiltrate the community. Paul's letter to the church in Colosse arms believers against the Gnostic heresy, one aspect of which is that the Incarnation couldn't have occurred since God wouldn't soil himself with tainted matter. False teaching is heinous in that in light of it Jesus Christ can't be called upon in faith, with the result that He can't be known; and neither can He then claim the obedience of those whose lives He longs to shape. In short, doctrinal standards do much to resist that false teaching which imperils people concerning their salvation and their discipleship.

(3) Doctrinal standards help the Church in determining the parameters for church membership and for holding office within the Church. While the gospel orients the Church both to Jesus Christ and to the world for which He came, Church and world are not the same. Regardless of the service the Church renders the world and must render it, the Church can render such a service only as long as the Church is different from the world *and knows wherein it differs.*

In the same way those who hold office and thereby exercise leadership within the Church must be able to say "I know whom I have believed" (2 Timothy 1:12)—and thereafter assist others in growing up into Christ Jesus. It is the apostle's purpose to present every man and woman "mature in Christ" (Colossians 1:28). This can be done only as the Church insists that its leaders have an adequate grasp of doctrine.

(4) Doctrinal standards assist the Church in its theological and institutional engagement with the genuine, creaturely wisdom of academic disciplines. Psychology, sociology, neurology, biology, anthropology, psychiatry, literature, music, drama, dance—all

of these provide an angle of vision on what it means to be a human being. We neglect these at our peril. A church that dismisses them peremptorily advertises its silliness, shrillness, folly and ingratitude to God. At the same time, while such disciplines provide *an* angle of vision—while they describe the human situation—neither individually nor collectively can they approach the human condition. At the same time, the Church must always recognize the nature of the relationship between situation and condition, and be able to speak to both—even as the Church remains aware of where and how different disciplines move illegitimately beyond their own expertise and encroach upon the preserve of theology.

Doctrinal standards will ever be essential to the Church's identity, preservation and usefulness in accord with its commission.

Printed in the United States
104098LV00002B/1-24/A